Where is Nuddly?

Written and illustrated by
Christine Davis

© Footsteps Publishing Limited 1984
ISBN 1 85045 000 5

This is Nancy.

C

This is her Mummy, who is very busy.
She works in the shop
at the end of the road.

For a whiter wash!
BOZ
recommended by all leading makes of washing machine

6p off Waggy Tail!

16·31
Kasho
C

This is her Daddy, who is busy too.
He is a milkman.

c

This is Sweet Sue, Nancy's sister,
who never wears skirts.
Sweet Sue is seven and goes to school
every day.

And this is Nuddly.
Some children like to suck their thumbs.
Some like to cuddle their teddy.
Others like to suck a dummy,
but Nancy has Nuddly.

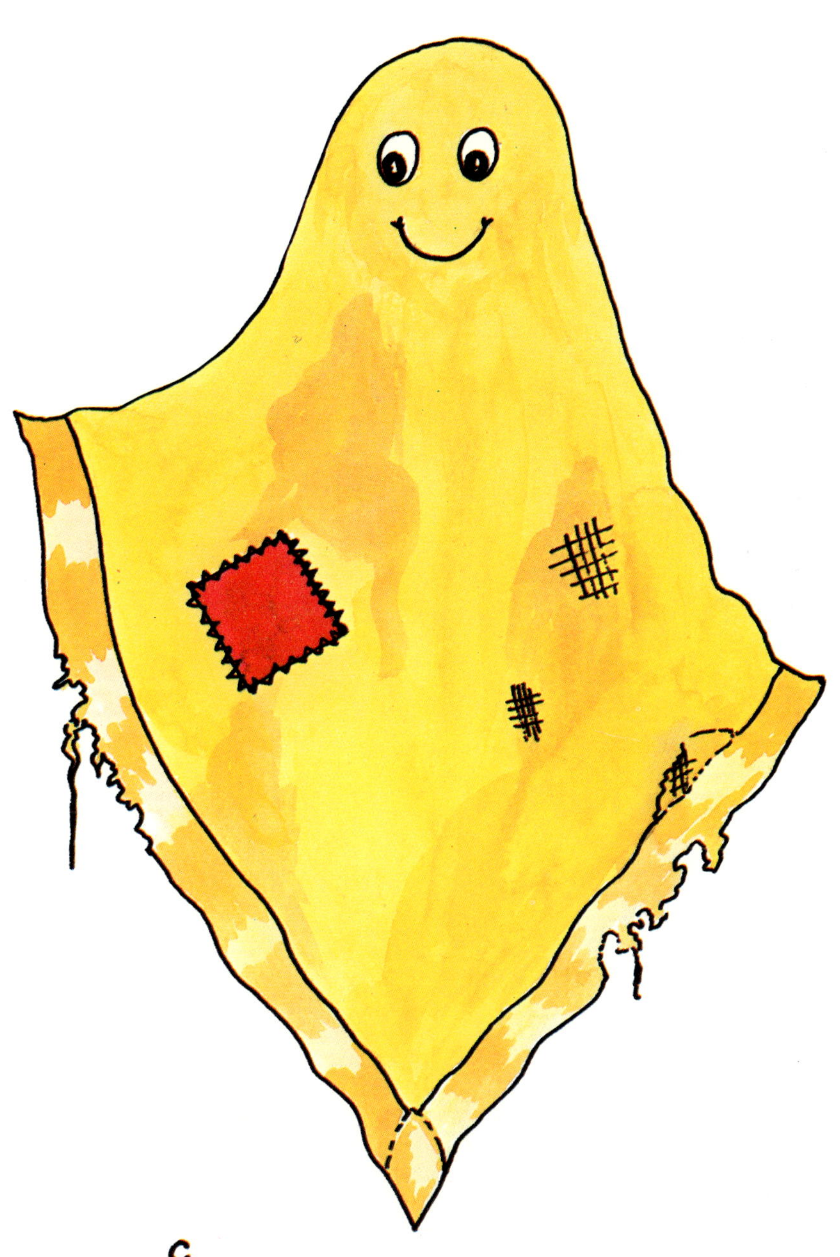

c

Nuddly is made from Nancy's old
blanket.
When Nancy was new,
Nuddly was new.

Now Nancy is three, and so is Nuddly.

Goodnight, Gorgeous!

Whenever Nancy feels sad,
Nuddly is a great comfort.

When Nancy is happy,
Nuddly always smiles.

Oh good!
Sweet Sue's
back from
school.

Nancy plays with Nuddly and often
forgets where she left him.

One night when it was Daddy's turn to
put the children to bed, Nancy asked
a most important question

Oh no!
Not again!

Where's
Nuddly,
Daddy?

They looked in the bed.
They looked in the toy box.
They searched everywhere for
Nuddly.

Can you see where Nuddly is?

Well –
when did you
last have it?

Suddenly Nancy remembered
she'd given Nuddly
a ride in Daddy's pocket.

Look, Daddy!
C

Goodnight Nancy.
Goodnight Nuddly.
Sleep well!